fraction jugglers

The Fraction Chart

The Fraction Chart helps you compare the sizes of different fractions. The bars at the top and bottom of the chart each stand for ONE WHOLE. The seven other bars are cut into fractional parts.

We hope you'll keep this page open and use the Fraction Chart as you read through the book and play the games. Whenever you see this symbol **USE THE FRACTION CHART**, it means we think the chart may be especially helpful.

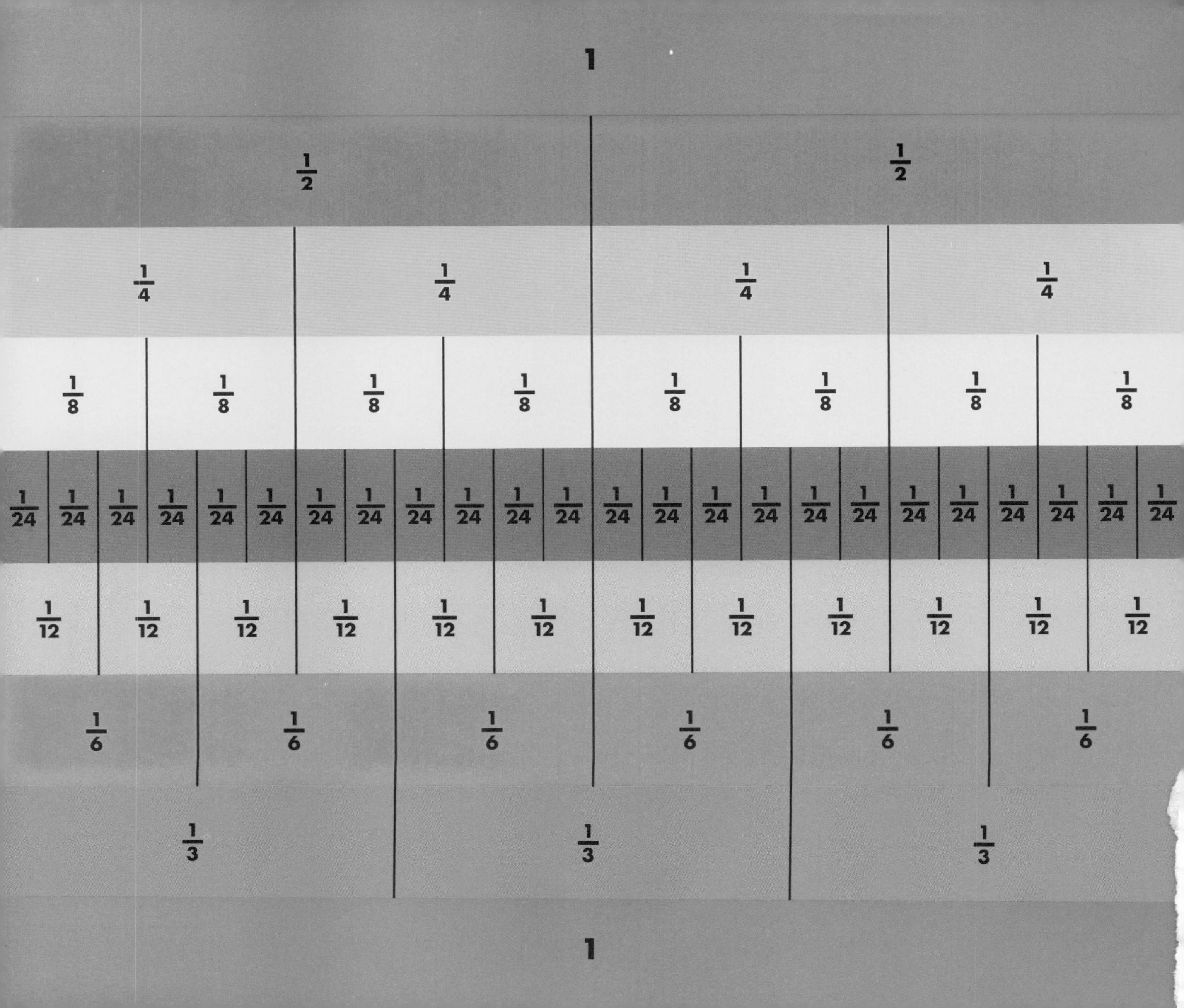
1
1/2 1/2
1/4 1/4 1/4 1/4
1/8 1/8 1/8 1/8 1/8 1/8 1/8 1/8
1/24 1/24 1/24 1/24 1/24 1/24 1/24 1/24 1/24 1/24 1/24 1/24 1/24 1/24 1/24 1/24 1/24 1/24 1/24 1/24 1/24 1/24 1/24 1/24
1/12 1/12 1/12 1/12 1/12 1/12 1/12 1/12 1/12 1/12 1/12 1/12
1/6 1/6 1/6 1/6 1/6 1/6
1/3 1/3 1/3
1

Fold out for the Fraction Chart

fraction jugglers

a math gamebook for kids + their parents

Ruth Bell Alexander

Illustrations by Tim Robinson

WORKMAN PUBLISHING • NEW YORK

Library of Congress Cataloging-in-Publication Data
Alexander, Ruth Bell.
    Fraction jugglers : a math gamebook for kids and their parents / by Ruth Bell Alexander ;
    illustrations by Tim Robinson.
        p. cm.
    ISBN 0-7611-2104-8 (alk. paper)
    1. Fractions—Study and teaching (Elementary)—Juvenile literature. 2. Games in
    mathematics education—Juvenile literature. [1. Fractions. 2. Mathematical recreations.]
    I. Title: Fraction card games. II. Robinson, Tim, 1963– ill. III. title.

QA117 .A54 2001
513.2'6—dc21   2001026098

Workman books are available at special discounts when purchased in bulk for premiums and
sales promotions as well as for fund-raising or educational use. Special editions can also be
created to specification. For details, contact the Special Sales Director at the address below.

Workman Publishing Company, Inc.
708 Broadway
New York, NY 10003-9555
www.workman.com

Manufactured in Hong Kong

First printing October 2001

10 9 8 7 6 5 4 3 2 1

Contents

Acknowledgments

Lila Schreiber, Tanner Arndt, and Azalea Miketti, three young friends who were starting fourth grade when I asked for their help, tested every game and read every word of the original manuscript. Their enthusiasm encouraged me. The incredible speed with which they picked up fraction concepts astounded me.

As always, I am deeply indebted to Judith Anne McBride and her terrific multi-age group of third and fourth graders at Lincoln School in Ashland, Oregon, for welcoming me and *Fraction Jugglers* into their classroom.

Thanks to my friend Sandy Wasserman, who read the manuscript carefully from the perspective of a nonmathematician, and to Brenda Paustian, a high school math teacher, who played the games with her son before there was even a manuscript to read.

Special thanks to Bea Carlson, also a math teacher, for being willing to answer all my questions, no matter at what time of day or night I called.

I would like to pay tribute to Angela G. Andrews, whose moral support has sustained me throughout this entire process. Her fourth- and fifth-grade students at Scott School in Naperville, Illinois, integrated *Fraction Jugglers* games into their lessons and e-mailed their comments to me with the swiftness of Olympic medalists. And I'm grateful to Angela's math professor husband, Bill, who was kind enough to check through the original manuscript for accuracy.

Liz Carey of Workman Publishing kept the project alive with her enthusiasm for the games, and Anne Kostick, formerly of Workman, helped get the project off the ground.

Finally, my husband David, who is actually able to manage any number of fancy calculations in his head, suspended all mathematical expertise to read these pages as if he were just learning about fractions for the first time. His suggestions more than once helped me to clarify complicated concepts.

As every writer knows, a manuscript may change daily. This one was no exception. Therefore, I take full responsibility for any errors that might be in these pages as it goes to press.

Preface for Parents and Teachers

Figuring things out in math is satisfying. It makes you feel smart. *Fraction Jugglers* is designed to help children feel smart about fractions. They may not know a fraction from a flagpole when they begin, but as they read through the book and play the games, they will build an understanding of how to use and manipulate fractions. By the end, we hope your kids will feel so smart about fractions that they'll consider themselves fraction experts.

Fraction Jugglers presents important fraction concepts as a preface to each game. New ideas are introduced slowly, with the intent of nipping confusion in the bud wherever possible, and more advanced material is introduced in sequence, after the fundamentals have been established.

The games are arranged according to how much knowledge of fractions is needed to enjoy playing them. The early games help beginners recognize and differentiate fractions. The middle games focus on comparing fraction sizes, combining fractions through adding and subtracting, and recognizing equivalent fractions. Toward the back of the book, more challenging games help players advance their skill at converting fractions to equivalent fractions with common denominators, changing mixed numbers to improper fractions, and multiplying and dividing fractions.

As with anything new, when young people go through the book for the first time, they will enjoy having you nearby for support. Parents and teachers can tailor the *Fraction Jugglers* games to meet each child's ability level. For example, with younger children who have not studied fractions, you might choose to have them play only the first two or three games and use only the $\frac{1}{2}$, $\frac{1}{3}$, and $\frac{1}{4}$ cards. Then, as your children's proficiency increases, they themselves will want to include other cards in their play. By the time they reach the final games in the book, they will be using all the cards and combining twelfths and thirds and eighths with ease. That's the goal!

Look for the Fraction Chart at the front of this book. It shows the relationship one fraction has to another and gives a graphic representation of fraction equivalencies. Players are welcome to use the Fraction Chart whenever they need it.

Note: The *Fraction Jugglers* deck does not contain operation signs—the addition, subtraction, multiplication, and division signs that tell us what to do in math. When kids see an operation sign their brains seize on it, and they stop inventing. For the games in this book, we want children to make whatever connections and relationships they can from their own store of knowledge. We want them to become creative math thinkers and, in the process, learn that math really is a lot of fun.

Introduction

Did you know that every time you bite into a slice of pizza, you're actually eating a fraction? And each time you drink a cup of milk, you're drinking a fraction? Fractions are everywhere. They're with us all the time. In fact, time itself is full of fractions. As the clock ticks off each minute, that's another fraction passing by.

Fractions are what you get when you divide something whole into equal-size parts.

Cut a pizza into 8 equal-size slices, and each one of the 8 slices is one eighth ($\frac{1}{8}$) of the whole pizza. There are 4 cups of milk in 1 quart, so each cup is one fourth ($\frac{1}{4}$) of the whole quart of milk. Since 60 minutes make an hour, each minute is one sixtieth ($\frac{1}{60}$) of an hour. No matter what "whole" we start with, if we divide it into equal-size parts, we're making fractions.

Think of a dollar. Do you know how many cents are in one whole dollar?

100 cents.

That's right. One dollar equals 100 cents. So how many cents are in half a dollar?

50 cents.

Yes! Divide a dollar into 2 equal amounts and you get 50 cents and 50 cents.

Each 50 cents is one half ($\frac{1}{2}$) of the whole dollar.

That's why the coin that is worth 50 cents is called a "half-dollar."

What about the coin that's called a "quarter"? What fraction of a dollar do you think that equals?

Is it $\frac{1}{4}$?

Absolutely! **A quarter is one fourth (one quarter) of a dollar.** How many cents is that?

If you don't already know the answer, you can figure it out by dividing 100 cents into 4 equal parts. How many cents are in each part?

25 cents.

So the coin that equals 25 cents is $\frac{1}{4}$ of a dollar.

And 1 cent is $\frac{1}{100}$ (one one-hundredth) of a dollar. Do you know why?

No. Why?

Because it takes 100 of them to make a whole dollar. In fact, our word "cent" comes from the Latin word that means one hundred.

You can use candy to learn about fractions, too. Say you have a whole chocolate bar that you and one friend want to share evenly. How much of the chocolate will each of you get?

$\frac{1}{2}$ each.

That's exactly right! You'll each get $\frac{1}{2}$ of the whole bar.

What if another friend comes along before you divide the chocolate, and you decide to let her have an equal share, too? Now how much will each of you get?

$\frac{1}{3}$?

CHOCOLATE

Yes! Since there are three people, you'll cut the bar into three equal pieces. Each person will get $\frac{1}{3}$ of the chocolate bar.

If four people want to share it, each person will get $\frac{1}{4}$ of the chocolate bar.

How much do you think each person will get if ten people want to share it?

Name That Fraction

Every fraction is made up of a number on top and a number on the bottom. The numbers are separated by a bar that stands for "divide." We'll talk more about that bar later.

Do you agree that the fraction $\frac{1}{4}$ looks very different from the fraction $\frac{5}{8}$? The top numbers are different, and the bottom numbers are different, too. What about the fractions $\frac{1}{4}$ and $\frac{1}{3}$? Are they the same or different?

Well, the top numbers are the same, but the bottom numbers are different, so $\frac{1}{4}$ and $\frac{1}{3}$ are not the same fraction. With fractions, we pay attention to the top number AND the bottom number.

When we say the name of a fraction, we say the top number first. The top number is called the **numerator** (NOO-mer-ay-ter).

Then we say the bottom number, called the **denominator** (dee-NAH-min-ay-ter), as if it were a floor in a building— for example, third, fourth, fifth, and so on.

The two fractions that don't follow that rule are halves and quarters. We call $\frac{1}{2}$ "one *half*," not "one *second*." The fraction $\frac{1}{4}$ can be called "one fourth," and it can also be called "one quarter."

$\frac{1}{2}$ **is called one half.**

$\frac{1}{3}$ **is called one third.**

$\frac{1}{4}$ **is called one fourth (or one quarter).**

$\frac{1}{5}$ **is called one fifth.**

$\frac{1}{6}$ **is called one sixth.**

$\frac{1}{7}$ **is called one seventh.**

$\frac{1}{8}$ **is called one eighth.**

What do you think $\frac{1}{9}$ is called?

One ninth?

Yes!

Fraction Rummy

Make sets of identical fractions and be the first to "go out."

How to Play

1. Each player takes a card; the one with the bottom number (denominator) closest to 1 goes first. Players return the cards to the deck and shuffle it. They are dealt eight cards each. The rest of the deck goes in the middle, fraction-side down.

2. The object of the game is to put all your cards into sets of identical fractions. You can have sets of two of a kind, three of a kind, or four or more of a kind. To go out, all your cards must belong to one set or another.

3. Player One takes one card from the middle. If she can use it to build a set, she keeps it and starts a discard pile by discarding another card from her hand. If she can't use the card she took, she may discard that card. Then it's Player Two's turn to take a card from the middle.

4. Player Two may take the top card from either the deck (which is facedown, so players don't know what the top card is) or the discard pile (which is faceup). Then Player Two discards one of his cards onto the discard pile. If more than two people are playing, Players Three and Four do the same.

5. Play continues until one player "goes out," which means she can put down all of her cards into sets of two, three, four, or more of a kind. She may use her ninth card in a set when she goes out, or she may discard it and go out with eight cards.

6. Players get 10 points for going out; 5 points for each set of two; 10 points for each set of three; 15 points for each set of four; 20 points for each set of five; and so on.

7. The players who didn't go out get points (as in rule 6) for any sets they have in their hands. They must then subtract 2 points for every card in their hand that is not in a set.

8. Players keep track of their points and continue playing until one player reaches 100 points.

Fabulous Fraction Fact #1

The bottom number of a fraction is the denominator (dee-NAH-min-ay-ter). It tells how many pieces the whole amount has been divided into.

• •

The word *denominator* comes from "denominate," which means "to give a name to something." Fractions get their name from the number of equal pieces in the whole amount. Here's how it works:

Say you start with a pie. That's the "whole." If you cut that pie into 6 equal pieces, each piece is called $\frac{1}{6}$ (one sixth) of the whole pie.

With the fraction $\frac{1}{6}$, the denominator (the number on the bottom) tells us:

This whole has been cut into 6 equal pieces.

Divide an hour into 2 equal segments of time.

Each segment is $\frac{1}{2}$ (one half) of an hour. The denominator 2 tells us:

This whole is in 2 equal parts.

If the whole is a dozen (12) eggs, each egg is $\frac{1}{12}$ (one twelfth) of the dozen. The denominator 12 says:

This whole has 12 equal portions.

The Denominator Game

The denominator is the BOTTOM number of the fraction. In this game players ask for fractions by denominator.

How to Play

1. Each player takes one card. The player with the bottom number (denominator) closest to 1 is Player One and goes first. Player One gathers the cards, shuffles them, and deals eight cards to each player. Players should keep their cards private.

2. Player One asks Player Two for a denominator. Example: "Do you have any fourths?" Player One can only ask for fourths if he has at least one card with 4 in the denominator in his hand. If Player Two has cards with 4 in the denominator, she must give **all** of them to Player One.

3. Player One puts those cards with his own cards of that denominator and places them in a separate pile. Both sides must start each turn with eight cards, so if they need to, after each turn they take enough cards from the deck to make eight.

4. Now Player Two asks for a denominator. For example: "Do you have any eighths?" If Player One has eighths, he must give all of them to Player Two, who puts them together with her own eighths to save in her pile. Then both players pick up enough cards from the deck to make eight in hand.

5. If a player asks for a denominator that his opponent doesn't have, his turn is over. No cards are taken from the deck. A player may not add to his pile unless he asks for and receives cards from his opponent.

6. If neither player has any of the cards the other needs, they both trade in two of their cards for two new cards from the deck to keep the game going.

7. Players play back and forth until there are no cards left in the deck. To give each player an equal number of turns, Player Two must have the last turn asking.

8. Players count the cards in their pile of saved cards and **subtract** from that the number of cards still in their hands. That's their score. Whoever has the highest score wins the game.

That's Great

Question: Who's bigger, Mr. Bigger or Mr. Bigger's baby?

Answer: Mr. Bigger's baby. She's a little Bigger.

• •

There's a funny thing about fractions. If two fractions come from equal-size whole amounts, and if those two fractions have the *same* number on top, then the fraction with the GREATER NUMBER on the bottom is actually the SMALLER AMOUNT!

Look at the pies in the picture and see if you can figure out why that is.

The more pieces a pie is cut into, the smaller each piece is.

That's why if I were hungry and someone offered me $\frac{1}{4}$ or $\frac{1}{12}$ of a cherry pie, I'd choose $\frac{1}{4}$. It's a lot more pie than $\frac{1}{12}$.

Of course, a lot depends on what size "whole" you start with!

When you play the next game, imagine that all the fractions come from whole amounts that are exactly the same size.

The What's Greater? Game

The object is to compare your cards to your opponents' cards. The greater amount wins the cards. That means the card with the denominator closest to 1 wins the cards. **USE THE FRACTION CHART**

How to Play

1. Remove from the deck all cards that **don't** have 1 as the top number and set them aside. Shuffle the remaining cards and divide them evenly between the players. (Set aside any extras.) Players keep their cards in a pile, number-side down.

2. The players turn over their top card at the same time. The player with the greatest amount (the denominator closest to 1) wins the cards. The winning player keeps those cards in a separate pile.

3. If players turn over the same fraction, they each turn over another card. Whoever has the greater amount in this second turnover wins all the cards. Should the second turnover result in a match, they each turn over a third card. The winner takes all the cards.

NOTE: If three people are playing and two players have a match but the third player's fraction is the greatest, the third player takes the cards. No second turnover is needed. If the third player's fraction is smaller, the winner of the match takes that card, too.

Variation: Play this game again, but this time the *smaller* fraction amount wins each turn. (That's the denominator number farthest from 1.)

Challenge: You can also play this game using *all* the fraction cards. The fraction "pies" on your cards will help you compare fraction sizes. You can also use the Fraction Chart at the front of the book.

4. When all cards have been played, players count the cards they have won. The player with the most cards wins the game. (Or you can keep playing, using the cards in the pile you have won. Play until someone is out of cards.)

Fabulous Fraction Fact #2

In every fraction, the number above the denominator is the numerator (NOO-mer-ay-ter). It tells how many pieces of the whole we are talking about.

The denominator (the number on the bottom) tells us how many pieces the whole amount is divided into. The numerator (the number on top) tells us how many of those pieces we are referring to. **The numerator lets us know how close we are to having ALL the pieces.**

For example, if a pie has been cut into 8 pieces and I have 5 of those pieces, I have $\frac{1}{8} + \frac{1}{8} + \frac{1}{8} + \frac{1}{8} + \frac{1}{8}$ of the pie.

That's $\frac{5}{8}$ of the pie, 5 of the 8 pieces of the pie.

What happened to the other three pieces?

I think the clown wants to eat them.

The SMALLER the Better Game

Players win cards if their card has the SMALLER amount. **USE THE FRACTION CHART**

• • • • • • • • • • • • • • • • • • •

How to Play

1. Players take a card from the deck. The person with the smallest amount is Player One. Player One gathers all the cards and shuffles them. Next he places the deck, fraction-side down, in the middle so all players can see it. Finally he turns the top card over and starts a fraction-side-up pile with it. That's the Win Pile.

2. Now Player One picks the top card from the deck. If the fraction is a SMALLER amount than the fraction on the Win Pile, he wins his own card and the Win Pile, too. If it is the SAME fraction as the one that's showing, he places his card on the Win Pile and takes a new card. If his card is a GREATER amount than the Win Pile fraction, he leaves his card on the pile and does not get another card.

3. Cards are stacked on the Win Pile until someone wins the pile. Each time a player wins the pile, he turns over the next card from the deck to start another Win Pile.

4. Player Two takes a card from the deck and follows the directions in step 2. Third and fourth players do the same in turn.

5. Players continue until there are no more cards in the deck. All players must take the same number of turns.

6. Players count the cards they have won. The player with the most cards wins the game.

Fabulous Fraction Fact #3

When the numerator (top number) and the denominator (bottom number) are the same, the fraction equals 1 whole.

• •

The denominator (bottom number) of a fraction tells you how many pieces the whole is divided into. The numerator (top number) tells you how many of those pieces you are talking about.

When the numerator number is the same as the denominator number, that means you are talking about ALL the pieces—you are talking about ONE WHOLE.

When you get change for a dollar, you may end up with four quarters. Four quarters don't look like a dollar bill, but four quarters do equal the SAME AMOUNT as a dollar bill.

That's how fractions work, too. When the numerator and the denominator of a fraction are the same number, you have an amount that's equal to one whole.

4 cups of milk **=** $\frac{4}{4}$ of a quart of milk.

$\frac{4}{4}$ of a quart of milk **= 1** whole quart of milk.

4 quarters **=** $\frac{4}{4}$ of a dollar.

$\frac{4}{4}$ of a dollar **= 1** whole dollar.

12 eggs **=** $\frac{12}{12}$ of a dozen eggs.

$\frac{12}{12}$ of a dozen eggs **= 1** whole dozen eggs.

Of course, in order for fractional *objects* to make a whole amount, they have to start from the same type of whole object. $\frac{1}{4}$ cup of milk **+** $\frac{1}{4}$ of a dollar **+** $\frac{1}{4}$ of a pie **+** $\frac{1}{4}$ of a dozen eggs doesn't equal 1 whole anything!

But when fractions are used only as *numbers*,

$\frac{1}{4}$ **+** $\frac{1}{4}$ **+** $\frac{1}{4}$ **+** $\frac{1}{4}$ always equals $\frac{4}{4}$

and $\frac{4}{4}$ always equals the amount **1**.

$$\frac{4}{4} = 1$$

It's All in the Family

Every fraction in the world is part of a fraction family. The denominator (bottom number) tells us the name of the fraction family.

● ●

Fraction families are named for the number of equal-size parts needed to make 1 whole amount. For example, $\frac{1}{2}$ is part of the family of HALVES, $\frac{1}{4}$ is a member of the family of FOURTHS, and $\frac{1}{3}$ is from the family of THIRDS. What family do you think $\frac{1}{10}$ is from?

The **THIRDS** family **needs 3** equal parts to make 1 whole amount.

The **FOURTHS** family **needs 4** equal parts to make 1 whole amount.

The **TENTHS** family **needs 10** equal parts to make 1 whole amount.

That's good to know, because before we can join fractions by adding or subtracting, we have to know how many parts it takes to make 1 whole amount.

It's like putting together a jigsaw puzzle. We need a certain number of pieces to make the whole puzzle, and all those pieces must come from that same puzzle or they won't make the right picture.

When we put fractions together by adding or subtracting, **the fraction family tells us how many equal parts we need to make the whole amount.**

All the parts have to come from that same fraction family.

Fabulous Fraction Fact #4

To add or subtract fractions, the fractions must all have the same denominator (bottom number), **which means they must all come from the same fraction family.**

• •

When we add and subtract fractions, **the numbers in the numerator (the numbers on top) are the numbers we add and subtract.**

The denominator number stays the same throughout the whole operation. It reminds us of how many equal parts it takes to make the whole thing.

To practice adding and subtracting fractions, let's arrange these cards into families:

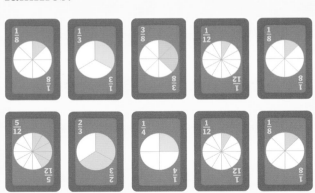

EIGHTHS:

THIRDS:

TWELFTHS:

And FOURTHS:

Let's add the EIGHTHS together:

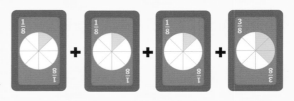

Remember, we add only the numbers in the numerator:

1 + 1 + 1 + 3

That equals 6.

The denominator tells us what fraction family we're adding, so the denominator stays the same: 8.

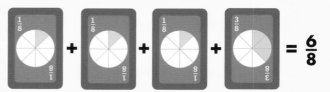

Our new, added-together amount is $\frac{6}{8}$, which means we have 6 parts from the family of EIGHTHS. (How many more parts do we need to make 1 whole?)

Now let's subtract the cards in the pile of THIRDS:

Remember, the denominator stays the same; we subtract only the numerators:

2 – 1 = 1

So  = $\frac{1}{3}$

Our new amount is $\frac{1}{3}$. That means we have 1 part from the family of THIRDS. (How many more parts do we need to make 1 whole?)

What if we subtract two fractions that are exactly the same? What do you think we get?

That's right.

When we subtract fractions that are equal to each other, we end up with zero.

$$\frac{1}{8} - \frac{1}{8} = \frac{0}{8}$$

or 0 parts of the family of EIGHTHS.

Zero!

The Fraction Jumble Game

Players try to add and subtract fractions
to make sets of 1 whole. **USE THE FRACTION CHART**

NOTE: You may want to play this
game on a large table or the floor
because you may have a lot of cards
spread out at the same time.

How to Play

1. Each player picks a card. The player with the denominator farthest from 1 goes first. Player One shuffles and deals out the deck evenly among the players. Players stack their cards facedown in front of them. Each player turns over his or her top card and places it in the middle, faceup.

2. Player One takes the top three cards from her pile and adds them faceup to the cards in the middle. She looks over the middle cards for fractions that she can add and/or subtract to equal 1 whole. She takes those cards to keep. She may make all the matches she sees. Example:

$$\frac{1}{3} + \frac{1}{3} + \frac{1}{3} = \frac{3}{3}$$

$$\frac{3}{3} = 1 \text{ whole.}$$

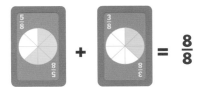

$$\frac{8}{8} = 1 \text{ whole.}$$

She keeps the cards she uses in a special pile to count at the end.

3. After each turn, if there are no cards left in the middle, every player must put in one card.

4. Now Player Two places three cards from his pile in the middle and looks for fractions that add up to 1 whole. He keeps the cards he uses.

5. A player may make ALL the wholes she sees in that turn. If a player cannot make any whole matches, she takes no cards. She leaves the unused cards faceup in the middle.

6. Players take turns laying down three cards per turn, then trying to add or subtract the fractions on the cards to make 1 whole. At the end, players count the cards they have kept. The player with the most cards wins.

How Big Is That, Anyway?

Which is more, 1 whole or $\frac{1}{2}$?

If fractions don't come from "wholes" of exactly the same size, they aren't going to match up.

So let's pretend we have two pizzas that are exactly the same size. Which do you think gives us more of the pizza: $\frac{3}{4}$ of the pizza or $\frac{5}{8}$ of the pizza?

That's right! If we have $\frac{3}{4}$ of a pizza, we need $\frac{1}{4}$ more of the pizza to make the pizza whole.

If we have $\frac{5}{8}$ of the other pizza, we need more than $\frac{1}{4}$ to make the pizza whole.

So $\frac{3}{4}$ gives us more pizza than $\frac{5}{8}$ does.

Now say we have two pizzas of exactly the same size, and we have $\frac{3}{4}$ of one and $\frac{7}{8}$ of the other.

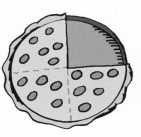 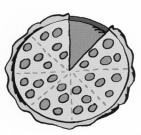

Which fraction gives us more pizza, $\frac{3}{4}$ or $\frac{7}{8}$?

Yes!
$\frac{7}{8}$ gives us more pizza.

As long as we start with items of the same size, $\frac{7}{8}$ is more than $\frac{3}{4}$.

Now think about this: Which gives us more pizza, $\frac{3}{4}$ or $\frac{6}{8}$?

Neither. They are both equal.

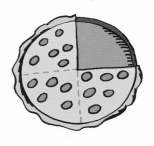 

Fabulous Fraction Fact #5

Two or more fractions can describe the same amount even though their numerators differ and their denominators differ.

● ●

To explain Fact #5, let's cut a banana cream pie into 8 pieces. Say my dog already ate 3 pieces. How many more pieces would he have to eat to have eaten one half ($\frac{1}{2}$) of the pie?

Okay, start from what you know. If the pie is cut into 8 pieces, it takes 8 pieces to make the whole pie.

So how many pieces does it take to make one half of the pie?

I don't know.

4 pieces?

Yes! If a pie is cut into 8 equal-size pieces ($\frac{8}{8}$), half of the pie is 4 pieces ($\frac{4}{8}$).

Another way to show that is:

$$\frac{4}{8} + \frac{4}{8} = \frac{8}{8} \text{ (1 whole)}.$$

So if my dog already ate 3 pieces ($\frac{3}{8}$ of the pie), how many more pieces would he have to eat to have eaten one half of the pie?

One more piece!

Yes! You see, $\frac{4}{8}$ of the pie is the same amount as $\frac{1}{2}$ of the pie.

I'm confused. How can $\frac{4}{8}$ be equal to $\frac{1}{2}$? They're not the same.

The answer is that they're not *written* the same way, but they equal the same amount.

Here's why: When we divide whole things into parts, there are *lots* of different ways to do the dividing. We can cut a pie into 2 equal parts, and each piece is $\frac{1}{2}$ of the pie, part of the family of HALVES.

Or we might cut the same pie into 4 equal parts, and each piece would be $\frac{1}{4}$ of the pie, part of the family of FOURTHS. How many pieces would it take to make one half of the pie now?

Two pieces!

That's right. $\frac{2}{4}$ is the same *amount* as $\frac{1}{2}$.

$$\frac{2}{4} = \frac{1}{2}$$

If we cut our pie into 6 equal parts, then each piece would be part of the family of SIXTHS. How many pieces would it take to make $\frac{1}{2}$ now?

Three pieces.

$\frac{3}{6}$ is the same amount as $\frac{1}{2}$.

$$\frac{3}{6} = \frac{1}{2}$$

The important idea to remember is that fractions describe amounts, and fractions from different families can describe the same amount.

Equivalent fractions belong to different fraction families but they show the same amount.

$\frac{1}{2}$ is the same amount as $\frac{2}{4}$ and $\frac{3}{6}$. So $\frac{1}{2}$, $\frac{2}{4}$, and $\frac{3}{6}$ are equivalent fractions.

Once we know how many parts it takes to make one whole, then we can figure out how many parts it takes to make part of the whole, such as one half.

A Half Is a Half Is a Half

Every fraction below is equivalent to all the others.

$$\frac{1}{2} \quad \frac{2}{4} \quad \frac{3}{6} \quad \frac{4}{8} \quad \frac{5}{10} \quad \frac{6}{12}$$

Each fraction above equals $\frac{1}{2}$. Look carefully at the numerators and denominators.

Can you see anything they all have in common?

No.

Well, look at the way the denominator (the bottom number) in all those fractions is exactly two times the size of the numerator (the top number).

One half is that way, too! The denominator, 2, is twice the size of the numerator, 1. The fraction $\frac{1}{2}$ says, "I have 1 out of 2 pieces, which means I have $\frac{1}{2}$ of the whole amount."

All fractions whose denominators are twice the size of their numerators tell us they are $\frac{1}{2}$ of the whole amount.

$\frac{2}{4}$ has 2 out of 4 pieces, which is the same as $\frac{1}{2}$ of the whole amount.

$\frac{3}{6}$ has 3 out of 6 pieces, which is the same as $\frac{1}{2}$ of the whole amount.

$\frac{50}{100}$ has 50 out of 100 pieces, which is the same as $\frac{1}{2}$ of the whole amount.

Now you can play the next game and get a lot more points than you would have if you thought one half could only look like this: $\frac{1}{2}$.

The Make $\frac{1}{2}$ Game

In each turn, teams try to make their cards into sets that equal $\frac{1}{2}$. **USE THE FRACTION CHART**

· ·

How to Play

1. Decide who goes first, then deal Team One ten cards faceup.

2. Team One looks its cards over and tries to find sets of fractions that when added to each other or subtracted from each other equal $\frac{1}{2}$.

3. Here's an example. Say your cards are:

Sets that equal $\frac{1}{2}$:

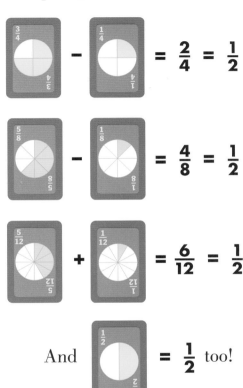

And 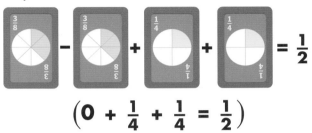 = $\frac{1}{2}$ too!

HINT: $\frac{1}{3} + \frac{1}{6}$ also equals $\frac{1}{2}$. Look on the Fraction Chart to see why.

4. Players may NOT get extra points by subtracting identical fractions to make zero, then adding or subtracting that from their sets. For example, you may NOT do this:

$$\left(0 + \frac{1}{4} + \frac{1}{4} = \frac{1}{2}\right)$$

5. Once Team One has arranged its cards into sets that equal $\frac{1}{2}$, the sets are put aside until the end of the game. Each card is worth one point. Players return their unused cards to the deck. Now Team Two is dealt ten cards and takes its turn.

6. Teams play back and forth until there aren't enough cards for both teams to have another turn. Then they count the cards they have kept. The team with the most cards wins the game.

What's in a Name?

nce upon a time, two jugglers, Billy and Millie, wanted to work out a new circus routine. They had a great idea—to juggle a dozen eggs between them. So they bought a dozen eggs, and each one took half the dozen home to practice.

Well, juggling half a dozen eggs is an almost impossible thing to do, and Billy was having a hard time keeping his eggs in the air. Every time he practiced, he broke three or four eggs.

In desperation, he asked his friend Tommy the Clown to help him. Billy was sure that with Tommy's help, the two of them could successfully juggle half a dozen eggs.

Tommy, always happy to oblige, came to practice the next day. Billy bought some replacement eggs and gave Tommy half of his $\frac{1}{2}$ of the dozen eggs, so they had $\frac{1}{4}$ dozen each. They worked and worked until those $\frac{2}{4}$ dozen eggs were passing from Billy to Tommy and back again with no mishaps.

The next day Millie brought her $\frac{1}{2}$ dozen eggs over. They practiced with them, and they didn't drop even a single egg. They all agreed that they had a really great act.

As they were getting ready to call it quits for the day, Billy, Tommy, and Millie went to put their eggs into the empty carton on the kitchen counter. "Uh-oh," said Billy. "What are we going to do? To put our eggs back into the same carton means that we have to add Millie's $\frac{1}{2}$ dozen to my $\frac{1}{4}$ dozen and Tommy's $\frac{1}{4}$ dozen eggs. Fabulous Fraction Fact #4 said we can only add and subtract fractions that have the same denominator."

"I guess we can't do it," said Millie unhappily.

"Oh yes we can," exclaimed Tommy. "All we have to do is call Millie's $\frac{1}{2}$ of the eggs another fraction name. Then we can add them together."

Do you know what they renamed Millie's $\frac{1}{2}$ of the eggs?

No. What?

Well, you might remember that the fraction $\frac{1}{2}$ is equivalent to lots of other fractions. $\frac{1}{2}$ equals $\frac{2}{4}$, $\frac{3}{6}$, $\frac{4}{8}$, $\frac{5}{10}$, and many, many, many more fractions. So Tommy renamed Millie's $\frac{1}{2}$ dozen eggs to an amount in the FOURTHS family, $\frac{2}{4}$ dozen eggs. Then he was able to add the eggs together.

$$\frac{2}{4} + \frac{1}{4} + \frac{1}{4} = \frac{4}{4}$$

$$\frac{4}{4} = 1$$

Since we're only allowed to add and subtract fractions that have the same denominator, **if we want to add or subtract fractions with different denominators we have to rename the fractions.** For a lot of games in this book, you'll get more points if you know how to rename fractions.

The Fraction Chart helps with renaming. From the chart you can see some of the fractions that are equal to each other. For example, look at your chart to see how many $\frac{1}{6}$s make the same amount as $\frac{1}{3}$.

Did you say that $\frac{2}{6}$ is the same amount as $\frac{1}{3}$? You're right. To add a $\frac{1}{3}$ card and a $\frac{1}{6}$ card, just rename $\frac{1}{3}$ to the family of SIXTHS: $\frac{2}{6}$. Then add:

$$\frac{2}{6} + \frac{1}{6} = \frac{3}{6}$$

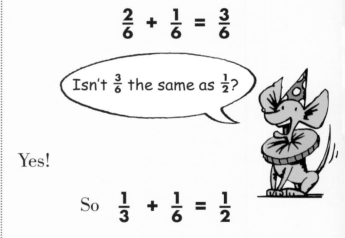

Isn't $\frac{3}{6}$ the same as $\frac{1}{2}$?

Yes!

So $\frac{1}{3} + \frac{1}{6} = \frac{1}{2}$

Check it out on the Fraction Chart to be sure.

The Fraction Chart helps with renaming, but we can rename fractions even without the chart. Remember: we want the **value** of the fraction to stay the same. We just want to change the fraction family. $\frac{1}{2}$ can be renamed $\frac{2}{4}$ because those two fractions equal each other—they both have the same value.

You probably already know that multiplying a whole number by 1 doesn't change the value of the number:

$$6 \times 1 = 6$$

$$43 \times 1 = 43$$

$$100 \times 1 = 100$$

Well, multiplying a fraction by 1 doesn't change its value either.

$$\frac{1}{2} \times 1 = \frac{1}{2}$$

That's the key to renaming fractions. **When we rename a fraction, all we do is multiply it by a special kind of 1, called a ONE fraction.**

What's a ONE fraction?

Look at Fabulous Fraction Fact #3.

When a fraction has the same number in the numerator as in the denominator, it is equal to 1.

$$\frac{5}{5} = 1$$

$$\frac{4}{4} = 1$$

$$\frac{8}{8} = 1$$

Well, a ONE fraction is a fraction that has the same number in its numerator as in its denominator.

If we want to rename $\frac{1}{2}$ to the family of SIXTHS—so that the renamed fraction has a 6 in the denominator—we have to find the right ONE fraction to do the job.

The first step is to think about the denominators. 2 is the denominator in $\frac{1}{2}$, and 6 is the denominator in the SIXTHS family. How can we go from a 2 in the denominator to a 6 in the denominator without changing the value of $\frac{1}{2}$?

I don't know.

We do it by multiplying $\frac{1}{2}$ by a ONE fraction that will change 2 to 6.

2 times what number equals 6?

I know. 3! 2 × 3 = 6!

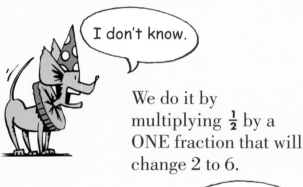

Yes! So our ONE fraction has 3 in the denominator. And if our ONE fraction has 3 in the denominator, it HAS to have 3 in the numerator too. Otherwise it won't equal 1.

$$\frac{3}{3} = 1$$

To rename $\frac{1}{2}$ to the SIXTHS family all we do is multiply $\frac{1}{2} \times \frac{3}{3}$.

$$\frac{1}{2} \times \frac{3}{3} = \frac{1 \times 3}{2 \times 3} = \frac{3}{6}$$

It's really pretty simple. To rename any fraction, first **find out how much you have to multiply the denominator by to change it to the new denominator, then multiply the numerator by the same number.** That will give you the renamed fraction.

Now that you know how to rename fractions, you can try your hand at the next games. Of course you can use the Fraction Chart to help you. The following samples will help you practice.

Say you have a $\frac{5}{6}$ card and you want to subtract $\frac{1}{3}$ from it. Can you do that?

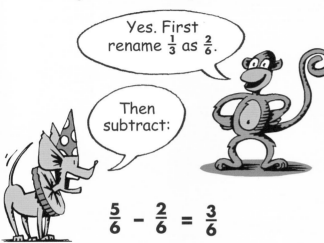

Yes. First rename $\frac{1}{3}$ as $\frac{2}{6}$.

Then subtract:

$$\frac{5}{6} - \frac{2}{6} = \frac{3}{6}$$

Can you add these five cards?

It's easy! That's $\frac{3}{6} + \frac{2}{4}$.

You can see on the Fraction Chart that both $\frac{3}{6}$ and $\frac{2}{4}$ can be renamed to the HALVES family.

So adding

is the same as adding $\frac{1}{2} + \frac{1}{2}$.

$$\frac{1}{2} + \frac{1}{2} = 1$$

Now what if you want to subtract a card from that answer?

How can I subtract $\frac{2}{3}$ from 1?

Just remember Fabulous Fraction Fact #3:

When the numerator and the denominator of a fraction are the same, the fraction equals 1 whole.

We can rename 1 whole into ANY fraction whose numerator and denominator are the same: $\frac{1}{1}$ and $\frac{2}{2}$ and $\frac{3}{3}$ and $\frac{4}{4}$ and $\frac{5}{5}$ and $\frac{6}{6}$ and $\frac{7}{7}$ and $\frac{8}{8}$ . . . $\frac{26}{26}$ . . . all equal 1.

So if we have 1, we can rename it into the family of THIRDS by calling it $\frac{3}{3}$.

I get it. Now we can subtract $\frac{2}{3}$ from $\frac{3}{3}$.

That's right!

$$\frac{3}{3} - \frac{2}{3} = \frac{1}{3}$$

The answer is $\frac{1}{3}$.

When a fraction is renamed to a family with a smaller number in the denominator, we call that simplifying the fraction. Instead of multiplying by a fraction that equals 1, we divide by a fraction that equals 1. We'll talk more about simplifying fractions on page 70.

The Renaming Game

FOR TWO TO FOUR PLAYERS

Players add and subtract fractions to equal Target Fractions. USE THE FRACTION CHART

How to Play

1. Players decide who goes first. Player One shuffles the deck, deals himself ten cards, faceup, and places the rest of the deck in the middle, fraction-side down.

2. Player One turns over the top card from the deck. That becomes his Target Fraction. He tries to add and/or subtract two or more of his ten cards to equal the Target Fraction. For example, if his Target Fraction is ⅓ and he has these cards:

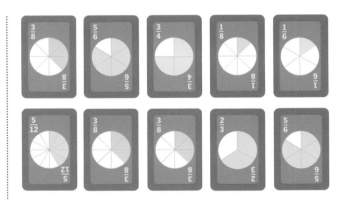

he might make ⅓ this way:

$$\frac{3}{8} + \frac{1}{8} - \frac{1}{6} = \frac{1}{3}$$

Player One keeps his three cards and wins the Target Fraction card. He sets all four cards aside in a Win Pile.

3. Player One turns over the next Target Fraction from the deck and tries to equal that with his remaining cards. If he succeeds, he keeps those cards and the Target Fraction, and turns over the next Target Fraction card. His turn lasts until he cannot make the next Target Fraction.

4. Each card may be used only ONCE. When a player's turn is over, he returns any unused cards to the deck. Players who are not able to make their first Target Fraction return all their cards and forfeit that turn.

5. Deal ten cards to Player Two. She repeats the game. Her turn lasts until she cannot make the next Target Fraction.

6. Each player gets three turns. The player who has won the most cards wins the game.

Family Matters

Some fraction families are directly related to each other and some aren't.

· ·

With the Fraction Chart we can see how a lot of fractions can be renamed. But we can't see every one. For example, if we want to add a $\frac{1}{3}$ card to a $\frac{1}{8}$ card, the chart doesn't show how many THIRDS equal EIGHTHS. Do you know why?

No, why?

Because fractions have to be directly related to each other before they can be renamed to each other's families.

How can you tell if fractions are directly related?

The denominators of fractions that *are* directly related divide into exactly the same number of parts.

Take $\frac{1}{3}$ as an example. The denominator of $\frac{1}{3}$ is 3. That denominator says: "My family divides into 3 equal parts."

There are many fraction families that also divide into three equal parts.

For example, you can see from the drawings below that the SIXTHS family divides into six equal parts, and it also divides into three equal parts. The NINTHS family divides into nine equal parts, and it also divides into three equal parts.

SIXTHS and NINTHS are directly related to THIRDS because they can be divided into three equal parts. That's why THIRDS can be renamed to SIXTHS and NINTHS.

$$\frac{1}{3} = \frac{2}{6} \quad \text{and} \quad \frac{1}{3} = \frac{3}{9}$$

$$\frac{2}{3} = \frac{4}{6} \quad \text{and} \quad \frac{2}{3} = \frac{6}{9}$$

$$\frac{3}{3} = \frac{6}{6} \quad \text{and} \quad \frac{3}{3} = \frac{9}{9}$$

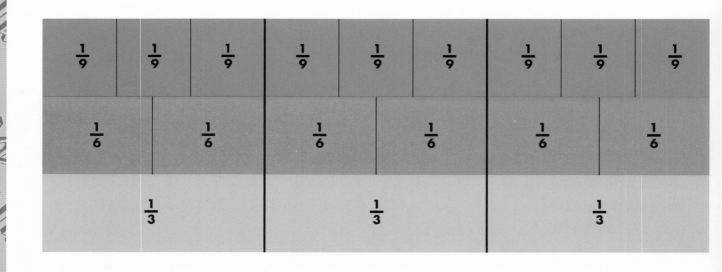

But the EIGHTHS family cannot be divided into exactly three *equal* parts, so $\frac{1}{3}$ *cannot* be renamed into EIGHTHS. EIGHTHS and THIRDS do not match up part for part.

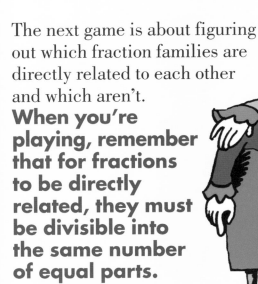

The next game is about figuring out which fraction families are directly related to each other and which aren't. **When you're playing, remember that for fractions to be directly related, they must be divisible into the same number of equal parts.**

For example, if you have a $\frac{3}{4}$ card and a $\frac{1}{12}$ card, TWELFTHS can be divided into exactly four equal parts, so FOURTHS and TWELFTHS are directly related.

With a $\frac{1}{6}$ card and a $\frac{1}{4}$ card, SIXTHS can't be divided into exactly four equal parts. So SIXTHS and FOURTHS are not directly related to each other.

The Family Matters Game

Players match fraction families whose
DENOMINATORS are related. **USE** THE FRACTION CHART

REMEMBER: Fractions are directly related if one denominator can divide into exactly the same number of parts as the other denominator, without any remainder.

How to Play

1. Use two cards each of $\frac{1}{2}$, $\frac{1}{3}$, $\frac{1}{4}$, $\frac{1}{6}$, $\frac{1}{8}$, and $\frac{1}{12}$ to make the Family Deck. The remaining cards are the Main Deck. Shuffle each deck and place them side by side in the middle of the players.

2. Decide who goes first. Player One turns over the top card of the Family Deck. The denominator (bottom number) of that card names the fraction family for Player One's entire turn.

3. Player One then turns over the top card of the Main Deck. If the two fractions are directly related, she keeps the card and turns over the next card in the Main Deck. If that card is also directly related to the family card, she keeps that card, too, and turns over the next card in the Main Deck.

4. Player One's turn continues until she turns over a card that is not directly related to her fraction family. For example: If the family card is $\frac{1}{8}$ and she turns over a $\frac{5}{6}$ card, her turn is over because SIXTHS and EIGHTHS are not directly related.

5. Now Player Two turns over a new card from the Family Deck. That denominator becomes the fraction family for his turn. He turns over the top card of the Main Deck; if it is directly related to his fraction family, he keeps the card and goes again. His turn lasts until he turns over a card that isn't directly related to his fraction family.

6. When the whole Family Deck has been used, players shuffle it and reuse it. The game continues until each player has had the same number of turns and there aren't enough cards to continue playing.

7. Players count the cards they have won. The player with the most cards wins the game.

Finding the Common Family

> If fraction families aren't directly related, we can find a common fraction family for them.

If you were thinking that there must be some way to add $\frac{1}{3}$ and $\frac{1}{8}$, you were right. THIRDS and EIGHTHS aren't related to each other. So before we can add them together, we have to rename them *both* to a fraction family that is related to both of them. We have to find a family that can be divided into 3 equal parts AND into 8 equal parts. That's their **common fraction family**. Read the two new Fabulous Fraction Facts to find out how.

Fabulous Fraction Fact #6

Before you can add or subtract fractions with different denominators, you must rename them to a COMMON FRACTION FAMILY to give them a common denominator.

• •

Every single group of fractions that you might ever want to add or subtract has a common fraction family.

Sometimes fractions are directly related, so it's pretty easy to find their common family. Look at FOURTHS and HALVES, for instance.

$$\frac{1}{2} \times \frac{2}{2} = \frac{1 \times 2}{2 \times 2} = \frac{2}{4}$$

$\frac{2}{4} + \frac{1}{2} + \frac{1}{2}$ can be renamed to $\frac{2}{4} + \frac{2}{4} + \frac{2}{4}$

$$\frac{2}{4} + \frac{2}{4} + \frac{2}{4} = \frac{6}{4}$$

Sometimes it's not so obvious what common family the fractions belong to, but if you know where to look, you can find out. **The best place to look for common families is on the multiplication tables!** (So if you don't already know your multiplication facts, this is a good time to learn them!)

To find the common family for $\frac{1}{3}$ and $\frac{1}{8}$, we look for all the families that can be divided into 3 equal parts and all the families that can be divided into 8 equal parts. Below is the 3s family:

Pick any answer number in the 3s table (3, 6, 9, 12, 15, 18, . . . 45 . . .) and try dividing it into three equal parts.

For example, how about 15:

$$15 \div 3 = 5$$

Fifteen can be divided exactly into 3 equal parts with 5 in each part. That means that

$$3 \times 5 = 15$$

The truth is, ALL the answer numbers (they're called "products") on the 3s

The 3s

The families that can be divided into 3 equal parts are on the 3s multiplication table:

$3 \times 1 = 3$	$3 \times 4 = 12$	$3 \times 7 = 21$	$3 \times 10 = 30$	$3 \times 13 = 39$
$3 \times 2 = 6$	$3 \times 5 = 15$	$3 \times 8 = 24$	$3 \times 11 = 33$	$3 \times 14 = 42$
$3 \times 3 = 9$	$3 \times 6 = 18$	$3 \times 9 = 27$	$3 \times 12 = 36$	$3 \times 15 = 45$

and on and on.

multiplication table are numbers that can be divided into 3 equal parts with nothing left over.

It's the same with EIGHTHS. All the products (answers) on the 8s multiplication table are numbers that can be divided into 8 equal parts with nothing left over.

The common family for $\frac{1}{3}$ and $\frac{1}{8}$ is a family that's on the 3s multiplication table AND on the 8s multiplication table.

(HINT: Look for the lowest product that's on both tables because that will make renaming easier.)

The 8s

The families that can be divided into 8 equal parts are on the 8s multiplication table:

$8 \times 1 = 8$	$8 \times 4 = 32$	$8 \times 7 = 56$	$8 \times 10 = 80$	$8 \times 13 = 104$
$8 \times 2 = 16$	$8 \times 5 = 40$	$8 \times 8 = 64$	$8 \times 11 = 88$	$8 \times 14 = 112$
$8 \times 3 = 24$	$8 \times 6 = 48$	$8 \times 9 = 72$	$8 \times 12 = 96$	$8 \times 15 = 120$

and on and on.

How about 24?
3 × 8 = 24 and
8 × 3 = 24.

Yes! Both THIRDS and EIGHTHS can be renamed to TWENTY-FOURTHS, which means 24 is a common denominator of $\frac{1}{3}$ and $\frac{1}{8}$.

HINT: Sometimes a good way to find the common denominator is to multiply the denominators together. Multiply the denominators of $\frac{1}{3}$ and $\frac{1}{8}$.

$$3 \times 8 = 24$$

You can see from the Fraction Chart at the front of the book that it takes more than just $\frac{1}{24}$ to equal $\frac{1}{3}$. It takes more than

just $\frac{1}{24}$ to equal $\frac{1}{8}$. $\frac{1}{3}$ is the same amount as $\frac{8}{24}$. $\frac{1}{8}$ is the same amount as $\frac{3}{24}$.

Now we can finally add $\frac{1}{3}$ and $\frac{1}{8}$. Rename

$$\frac{1}{3} + \frac{1}{8} \text{ to } \frac{8}{24} + \frac{3}{24}$$

Then add:

$$\frac{8}{24} + \frac{3}{24} = \frac{11}{24}$$

But without the chart, how do you know what numbers to put in the numerators?

Fabulous Fraction Fact #7 has the answer.

Fabulous Fraction Fact #7

To rename a fraction to a common family, you MULTIPLY its numerator and its denominator by the same number.

● ●

To rename any fraction, we multiply it by a ONE fraction. To rename $\frac{1}{3}$ into an equivalent fraction in the TWENTY-FOURTHS family, we ask:

By what number do we multiply the denominator of $\frac{1}{3}$ to rename it to TWENTY-FOURTHS?

3 x ? = 24

Well, from the multiplication tables, we know that $3 \times 8 = 24$. We also know that if the denominator of the ONE fraction is 8, the numerator has to be 8, too. So now we can convert $\frac{1}{3}$ to TWENTY-FOURTHS this way:

$$\frac{1}{3} \times \frac{8}{8} = \frac{1 \times 8}{3 \times 8} = \frac{8}{24}$$

It's the same with $\frac{1}{8}$. By what number do we multiply the denominator of $\frac{1}{8}$ to rename it to TWENTY-FOURTHS?

$$8 \times ? = 24$$
$$8 \times 3 = 24$$

The denominator of the ONE fraction is 3. So the numerator also has to be 3. Now we can convert $\frac{1}{8}$ to TWENTY-FOURTHS:

$$\frac{1}{8} \times \frac{3}{3} = \frac{1 \times 3}{8 \times 3} = \frac{3}{24}$$

The next game is a very good way to check out your renaming skills.

The Pass Game

● ●

How to Play

1. Deal two cards to each player.

2. Players look their cards over and pass one card to the person on their right.

3. Then everyone adds up the fractions on his or her cards by renaming them if necessary and finding common families.

4. Whoever has the highest amount wins everyone's cards.

5. If there is a tie, deal one more card to the tying players. They add that card to their other two. Whoever has the highest amount wins everyone's cards.

6. At the end of four rounds, the player with the most cards wins the game.

The More the Merrier

Can you add 2 or 3 or 4 fractions, all with different denominators?

· ·

If you want to add many fractions with different denominators, you do it the same way.

First rename ALL the fractions into one common family to give them a common denominator. Then you find the new numerators by multiplying each by a ONE fraction.

Let's try it with

$$\frac{3}{4} + \frac{5}{6} + \frac{1}{12}$$

Step 1. Find a common family for FOURTHS, SIXTHS, and TWELFTHS.

4s:	4, 8, **12**, 16, 20, 24
6s:	6, **12**, 18, 24, 30
12s:	**12**, 24, 36, 48

The products 12 and 24 are common to all three fractions. Since twelve is the least (or smallest) product common to all three fractions, TWELFTHS is the best common family, and 12 will be the common denominator.

> REMEMBER: When you're renaming fractions, look on the multiplication tables for the *smallest* common family you can find. That makes the renaming easier.

Step 2. Figure out what number you multiply the denominator by to rename the fraction:

$$4 \times 3 = 12$$
$$6 \times 2 = 12$$
$$12 \times 1 = 12$$

Step 3. Multiply both the numerator and the denominator by a ONE fraction of that number:

$$\frac{3}{4} \times \frac{3}{3} = \frac{3 \times 3}{4 \times 3} = \frac{9}{12}$$

$$\frac{5}{6} \times \frac{2}{2} = \frac{5 \times 2}{6 \times 2} = \frac{10}{12}$$

$$\frac{1}{12} \times \frac{1}{1} = \frac{1 \times 1}{12 \times 1} = \frac{1}{12}$$

Now you can add the fractions because they all have a common denominator:

$$\frac{9}{12} + \frac{10}{12} + \frac{1}{12} = \frac{20}{12}$$

If you've come this far, you are becoming a fraction expert! Have fun with the next two games!

The Winner Takes All Game

Players add their own cards together to try to win everyone else's cards.

• •

NOTE: To make the game less challenging, do not use the cards with 8 in the denominator.

How to Play

1. Players decide who goes first. One player shuffles the deck and deals each player three cards, facedown.

2. Players look at their cards privately and decide if they want to trade any in for new cards. Their goal is to make the highest score by adding their three cards together.

3. Players have one chance to trade in one, two, or all three of their cards for new cards from the deck if they want to. They need not trade any cards if they want to keep the ones they have.

4. After all the players have finished trading, they turn their cards over and add up their fractions. The player whose cards add up to the highest amount wins her own and everyone else's cards. She saves those cards in a Points Pile. At the end of the game, players will count the cards they have won.

5. If there is a tie, deal one more card to each tying player. Whoever has the highest sum wins. If they're still tied, deal another card to each player and compare the new sums.

6. Repeat the game until there aren't enough cards in the deck to keep playing. When the game is over, players count the cards in their Points Pile. Each card is worth 1 point. The player with the most points wins the game.

Variation: This game may also be played so that the person with the lowest sum wins each round. High sum or low sum must be decided before play begins.

The Take Your Chances Game

Players try to make their cards equal 1 whole.

● ●

NOTE: Use only the cards with 1 in the numerator. Remove all the other cards from the deck.

How to Play

1. Shuffle the deck and deal each player 2 cards, fraction-side down. Place the rest of the deck in the middle, fraction-side down.

2. Players review their cards privately. Then each has one turn to take from the deck, one card at a time, as many new cards as he wants; players may also choose not to take any new cards from the deck. Once a player has taken a card, he may not return it to the deck. The goal is to have your cards add up to 1 and NOT go over 1.

3. After all the players have had their chance to take new cards, they all turn their cards over. A player whose cards add up exactly to 1 wins his own and everyone else's cards. If no player has made exactly 1, the player whose cards come closest to but NOT OVER 1 wins everyone's cards. If there's a tie, winning players divide the cards evenly between them. If necessary, a card may be added from the deck to make it equal.

4. After each round, deal each player two new cards to repeat play. Repeat the game until not enough cards are left in the deck to play again.

5. Players count the cards they have won. Whoever has the most cards wins the game.

Challenge: Play this game using all the fraction cards and have the goal be to make 2 and not go over 2.

How Simple

When you're playing the *Fraction Jugglers* games, it helps to know about renaming fractions. It also helps to know about "simplifying" fractions. **USE THE FRACTION CHART**

If you want your fraction to equal the same amount but to have SMALLER numbers in its numerator and denominator, you DIVIDE the numerator and denominator by the same number. That's called *simplifying* the fraction.

Simplifying a fraction means finding an equivalent fraction with SMALLER numbers in its numerator and denominator. To rename fractions, we MULTIPLY the numerator and denominator by a ONE fraction.

To simplify fractions, we DIVIDE the numerator and the denominator by a ONE fraction.

Why would I want to simplify fractions?

Well, the easiest way to compare fractions is when they are in their simplest form. When you're playing some of the games in this book, you will want to compare fractions.

For example, if you come up with $\frac{16}{24}$ and your opponent comes up with $\frac{2}{3}$, who wins the game? If you know that 16 and 24 are both on the 8s multiplication table, you know both 16 and 24 can be divided by 8.

To simplify $\frac{16}{24}$ you divide it by the ONE fraction $\frac{8}{8}$:

$$\frac{16}{24} \div \frac{8}{8} = \frac{16 \div 8}{24 \div 8} = \frac{2}{3}$$

Presto! Now you know that $\frac{16}{24}$ is equal to $\frac{2}{3}$! You both win!

The easiest way to simplify fractions for the games in this book is to look on the Fraction Chart. If the fraction you want to simplify isn't on the chart, check out Fabulous Fraction Fact #8.

Fabulous Fraction Fact #8

A fraction can be simplified if it can be evenly DIVIDED by a ONE fraction other than $\frac{1}{1}$.

• •

We can simplify $\frac{16}{24}$ to $\frac{2}{3}$ because both 16 and 24 are products on the 8s multiplication table. That tells us the numerator (16) and the denominator (24) both have 8 as a factor.

To simplify fractions, we search for identical factors in the numerator and the denominator. Then we divide both the numerator and the denominator by a ONE fraction made from the largest of those factors.

What's a factor?

Facts About Factors

Let's use the number 12 to explain. What are the numbers that multiply together to make 12?

$1 \times 12 = 12$, so both 1 and 12 are factors of 12.
$2 \times 6 = 12$, so both 2 and 6 are factors of 12.
And $3 \times 4 = 12$, so both 3 and 4 are also factors of 12.

The numbers 1, 2, 3, 4, 6, and 12 are the factors of 12. They are the numbers that you multiply together to produce 12.

Factors are multipliers. They are also dividers. 12 can be divided evenly, without a remainder, by every one of its factors: 1, 2, 3, 4, 6, and 12.

$$12 \div 1 = 12 \qquad 12 \div 2 = 6 \qquad 12 \div 3 = 4$$
$$12 \div 12 = 1 \qquad 12 \div 6 = 2 \qquad 12 \div 4 = 3$$

To simplify $\frac{16}{24}$, we look at 16 and 24 to see if they have any factors in common.

$$1 \times 16 = 16$$
$$2 \times 8 = 16$$
$$4 \times 4 = 16$$

$$1 \times 24 = 24$$
$$2 \times 12 = 24$$
$$3 \times 8 = 24$$
$$4 \times 6 = 24$$

The factors of 16 are **1, 2, 4, 8,** and 16. The factors of 24 are **1, 2,** 3, **4,** 6, **8,** 12, and 24.

Do 16 and 24 have any factors in common?

Yes! They have 1, 2, 4, and 8 in common.

Okay, let's make those factors into ONE fractions and divide.

$$\frac{16}{24} \div \frac{1}{1} = \frac{16 \div 1}{24 \div 1} = \frac{16}{24}$$

$$\frac{16}{24} \div \frac{2}{2} = \frac{16 \div 2}{24 \div 2} = \frac{8}{12}$$

$$\frac{16}{24} \div \frac{4}{4} = \frac{16 \div 4}{24 \div 4} = \frac{4}{6}$$

$$\frac{16}{24} \div \frac{8}{8} = \frac{16 \div 8}{24 \div 8} = \frac{2}{3}$$

1 is a factor of every number. You can see, though, that the factor 1 doesn't really help us in simplifying fractions. **When we use 1 to divide our numerator and denominator, our fraction stays the same.**

The factors 2 and 4 do help simplify $\frac{16}{24}$, but they don't do a complete job.

We want to use the greatest common factor for our ONE fraction so that when we divide, there won't be any common factors left in our answer (except **1**). Since 8 is the greatest common factor for the fraction $\frac{16}{24}$, to simplify $\frac{16}{24}$ we divide its numerator and denominator by 8.

$$\frac{16}{24} \div \frac{8}{8} = \frac{16 \div 8}{24 \div 8} = \frac{2}{3}$$

Can every fraction be simplified?

No way! Some fractions can't be simplified because they're already in their simplest form.

A few of the fractions in their simplest form are $\frac{1}{2}$, $\frac{1}{3}$, $\frac{3}{8}$, $\frac{5}{12}$, $\frac{2}{3}$, $\frac{3}{4}$. There is no whole number other than 1 that can be evenly divided into the numerator and the denominator of those fractions.

come and see!
The Greatest Common Factor

The It's So Simple Game

Players make an equation to equal $\frac{1}{2}$, $\frac{1}{3}$, or $\frac{1}{4}$.

DEFINITION: An equation is a number sentence in which the amount on one side of the equal sign (=) equals the amount on the other side.

How to Play

1. Players take from the deck the $\frac{1}{2}$ cards, $\frac{1}{3}$ cards, and $\frac{1}{4}$ cards. Place the cards in the middle in three separate piles.

2. Players decide which team will go first and deal Team One ten cards from the deck.

3. By adding and subtracting their fractions, Team One's players try to make equations that simplify to $\frac{1}{2}$, $\frac{1}{4}$, or $\frac{1}{3}$. For example, if these are their cards:

Team One might make this equation to equal $\frac{1}{3}$:

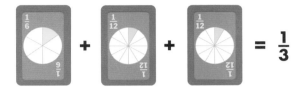

$$+ \quad + \quad = \frac{1}{3}$$

This works because $\frac{1}{6}$ can be renamed to $\frac{2}{12}$, and

$$\frac{2}{12} + \frac{1}{12} + \frac{1}{12} = \frac{4}{12}$$

$\frac{4}{12}$ simplifies to $\frac{1}{3}$. Team One takes a $\frac{1}{3}$ card to keep with the three cards it used to make $\frac{1}{3}$.

4. Team One's turn continues if they can make more equations. For example, they might make

$$- \quad - \quad = \frac{1}{2}$$

$\frac{3}{4}$ can be renamed to $\frac{6}{8}$, and

$$\frac{6}{8} - \frac{2}{8} = \frac{4}{8}$$

$\frac{4}{8}$ simplifies to $\frac{1}{2}$. So Team One takes a $\frac{1}{2}$ card to keep with the three cards it used to make $\frac{1}{2}$.

5. Each time a team makes an equation that simplifies to either $\frac{1}{2}$, $\frac{1}{3}$, or $\frac{1}{4}$, they take the appropriate card from the pile at the center and keep that with the cards they used to make the equation. In some games, one or more of the piles in the center may run out of cards. If that happens, teams no longer have the option to make equations to equal those fractions. A team's turn is over when it cannot make any more equations.

6. When both teams have had THREE turns to play, they count the cards they have kept. The team with the most cards wins the game.

The "I've Got It" Game

Players try to be the first to use their cards to equal the fraction in the middle.

• •

How to Play

1. The dealer shuffles the deck and deals seven cards to each player. Players use these same seven cards throughout the game. The dealer places the rest of the deck, fraction-side down, in the middle.

2. If a player is dealt more than two of the same fraction, he or she must trade them in for a different fraction.

3. Players arrange their seven cards, fraction-side up, in front of them on the floor or table where they are playing. Then one player turns over the top card from the deck in the middle. (Players take turns turning the top card over.)

4. Once players see the middle fraction, they try to be the first person to make an equation to equal it. They must use two or more of their cards, and they may use addition, subtraction, or both. The first player to equal the middle fraction slaps the deck and says, "I'VE GOT IT!"

5. The person who slaps the fraction tells the others her equation. If she is correct, she takes the middle fraction card to keep in a separate Win Pile till the end of the game. If she is incorrect, the other players have a chance to win the fraction.

6. A player who slaps the deck before having an equation must forfeit (give up) one card and continue playing with only six cards. If that player should slap early again, he or she must forfeit another card.

7. Keep playing until all the center cards have been won. At the end, the player with the most Win cards wins the game.

Variation: This is a fast and competitive game. If you prefer a slower game, take turns trying to equal the middle card instead of all competing at once.

That's Improper!

Proper fractions always equal less than one whole.

Fractions whose numerator is less than their denominator are called "proper" fractions.

$\frac{1}{2}$, $\frac{3}{4}$, $\frac{7}{8}$, $\frac{5}{12}$, and $\frac{99}{100}$ are all proper fractions. They equal an amount less than 1.

Often you'll have a fraction whose numerator is *greater* than its denominator. It's called an *improper* fraction. Improper fractions describe amounts that are greater than one whole.

Six thirds ($\frac{6}{3}$) is an example.

You know that in the family of THIRDS, it takes $\frac{3}{3}$ to make 1 whole. When you have $\frac{6}{3}$, you have enough for 2 wholes.

Do you remember that we said the bar between the numerator and denominator of a fraction means "divide"?

Fractions tell us about division. In fact, every fraction is a division problem. **Every fraction tells us to divide the amount in the numerator by the amount in the denominator.**

With improper fractions, because the numerator is larger than the denominator, when we divide the numerator by the denominator we always have more than one whole.

One, More or Less

When the numerator of the fraction is less than the denominator, the fraction equals less than 1. When the numerator of the fraction is the same as the denominator, the fraction equals 1. When the numerator is more than the denominator, the fraction equals more than 1.

Improper fractions can equal 2 or 3 or more wholes. With $\frac{6}{3}$, the denominator, 3, tells us that we need 3 parts to make one whole. The numerator, 6, tells us we have enough for two wholes because $6 \div 3 = 2$.

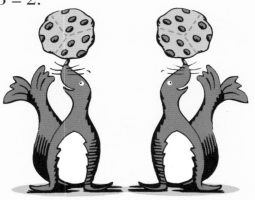

$$\frac{3}{3} + \frac{3}{3} = \frac{6}{3}$$

Some improper fractions equal a whole number plus a fraction. For instance, $\frac{4}{3}$ is like that.

$$4 \div 3 = 1\frac{1}{3} \ (\mathbf{1} \text{ and } \tfrac{1}{3})$$

Four thirds ($\frac{4}{3}$) is one whole ($\frac{3}{3}$) plus one third ($\frac{1}{3}$) more.

As you can see,

$$\frac{3}{3} + \frac{1}{3} = \frac{4}{3} \qquad \frac{4}{3} = 1\frac{1}{3}$$

When a fraction and a whole number are written together, we call that a mixed number.

The improper fraction $\frac{4}{3}$ equals the mixed number $1\frac{1}{3}$ (one and one third). There are lots of times when you'll use mixed numbers: if you're dividing up 5 cookies between 2 people ($\frac{5}{2}$), how many cookies will each person get?

You'll each get 2 whole cookies and a $\frac{1}{2}$ cookie!

Fabulous Fraction Fact #9

All whole numbers greater than 1 and all mixed numbers can be written as improper fractions.

• •

Say you have the whole number 3 and you want to know how many FOURTHS that equals. You have 3 wholes in the family of FOURTHS.

To rename 3 to the family of FOURTHS, multiply 3 times the denominator 4:

$$3 \times 4 = 12$$

So 12 is the new numerator. It tells you that 3 is the same amount as $\frac{12}{4}$.

$$3 = \frac{12}{4}$$

To rename any whole number greater than 1 as an improper fraction, all you do is multiply the whole number times the denominator, and the product becomes the new numerator.

Example: How many HALVES are 8?

$$8 \times 2 = 16$$

so

$$8 = \frac{16}{2} \text{ or sixteen halves.}$$

To rename a mixed number as an improper fraction, there are two steps:

Step 1. Change the whole number into a fraction with the same denominator as the fraction in the mixed number.

Step 2. Add that fraction to the fraction in the mixed number.

Now, try renaming **2$\frac{3}{5}$** (two and three fifths) as an improper fraction.

Step 1. Name 2 into the FIFTHS family by multiplying 2×5:

$$2 \times 5 = 10$$

That tells you that the whole number 2 equals $\frac{10}{5}$.

Step 2. Now add $\frac{10}{5}$ and $\frac{3}{5}$:

$$\frac{10}{5} + \frac{3}{5} = \frac{13}{5}$$

So **2$\frac{3}{5}$** equals the improper fraction $\frac{13}{5}$.

1 whole ($\frac{5}{5}$), another whole ($\frac{5}{5}$), and $\frac{3}{5}$

$$\frac{5}{5} + \frac{5}{5} + \frac{3}{5} = \frac{13}{5}$$

The Mix and Match Game

In each turn, players make a mixed number.

• •

NOTE: You need 8 items to use as markers (toothpicks, pens, or pencils). Keep score with pencil and paper.

How to Play

1. Players choose who goes first. One player shuffles the deck, then turns the top card over and places it in the middle to make the Goal Fraction for that turn. Player One is dealt fifteen cards, fraction-side up.

2. Player One uses his cards to equal the Goal Fraction AND as many whole numbers as he can make. Each card may be used only once. For example, say the Goal Fraction card is $\frac{3}{8}$ and Player One is dealt:

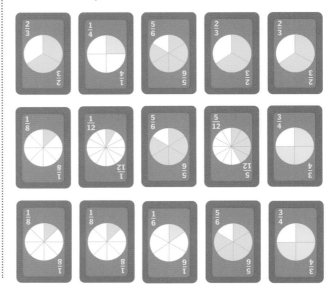

He may use his cards this way:

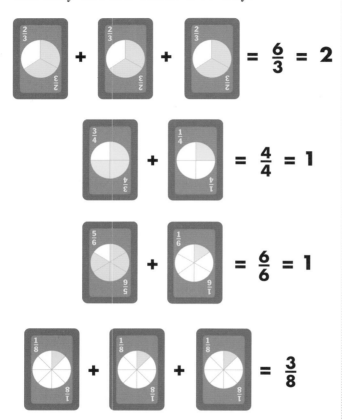

$$\frac{2}{3} + \frac{2}{3} + \frac{2}{3} = \frac{6}{3} = 2$$

$$\frac{3}{4} + \frac{1}{4} = \frac{4}{4} = 1$$

$$\frac{5}{6} + \frac{1}{6} = \frac{6}{6} = 1$$

$$\frac{1}{8} + \frac{1}{8} + \frac{1}{8} = \frac{3}{8}$$

Player One made 4 wholes plus $\frac{3}{8}$. That equals the mixed number **4$\frac{3}{8}$**.

3. For each whole amount a player makes, he takes a marker and places it next to the Goal Fraction in the middle. For **4$\frac{3}{8}$**, Player One puts four markers next to the $\frac{3}{8}$ card in the middle.

4. To score Player One's turn: In the example, he made **4$\frac{3}{8}$**. He multiplies the denominator of the Goal Fraction times the number of markers he used: $8 \times 4 = 32$. Then he adds that answer to the numerator of the Goal Fraction: $32 + 3 = 35$. His score for the first turn is 35.

5. Player One returns all his cards to the deck and his markers to the main pile of markers. He shuffles the deck and places the top card in the middle as the new Goal Fraction. Then he deals fifteen cards to Player Two for her turn.

6. Play goes on until one player reaches 100 points.

A Note on Parentheses

These curved lines, ( ), are called parentheses (puh-REN-thuh-sees). **Parentheses tell us what operations to perform first.**

Parentheses help us organize our numbers when we're solving math problems. For example, does $\frac{1}{2} - \frac{1}{12} + \frac{1}{4}$ equal $\frac{1}{6}$ or $\frac{2}{3}$? Where we put our parentheses determines our answer.

To solve $\frac{1}{2} - \frac{1}{12} + \frac{1}{4}$, we must put our fractions into a common family. TWELFTHS is the common fraction family for $\frac{1}{2}$, $\frac{1}{12}$, and $\frac{1}{4}$, because 12 is on the 2s, 4s, and 12s multiplication tables.

$$\frac{1}{2} = \frac{6}{12} \qquad \frac{1}{12} = \frac{1}{12} \qquad \frac{1}{4} = \frac{3}{12}$$

Now, we can either set up the equation this way:

$$\frac{6}{12} - \left(\frac{1}{12} + \frac{3}{12} \right) \;=\; \frac{6}{12} - \frac{4}{12} \;=\; \frac{2}{12} \quad \left(\frac{2}{12} \text{ simplifies to } \frac{1}{6} \right)$$

or we can set up the equation this way:

$$\left(\frac{6}{12} - \frac{1}{12} \right) + \frac{3}{12} \;=\; \frac{5}{12} + \frac{3}{12} \;=\; \frac{8}{12} \quad \left(\frac{8}{12} \text{ simplifies to } \frac{2}{3} \right)$$

We always have to do what's inside the parentheses before we add, subtract, multiply, or divide any other numbers.

The Make It Whole Game

Players add and subtract fractions to make WHOLE amounts. **USE THE FRACTION CHART**

• •

How to Play

1. Teams decide who goes first. Shuffle the deck and deal fifteen cards, faceup, to Team One.

2. Team One players add and/or subtract the fractions on their cards to make sets that equal whole numbers. Players may use their cards to make sets that exactly equal ANY whole number: 1, 2, 3, and so on.

Example:

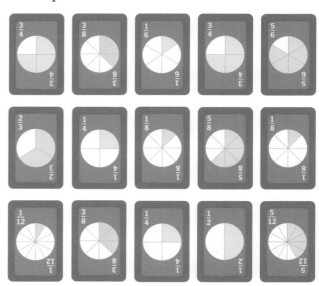

They might add

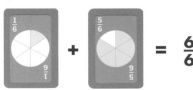 = $\frac{6}{6}$

$\frac{6}{6}$ equals 1 whole.

Next they might add

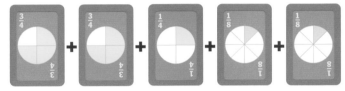

That equals $\frac{7}{4} + \frac{2}{8}$.

$\frac{2}{8}$ simplifies to $\frac{1}{4}$. So that's

$$\frac{7}{4} + \frac{1}{4} = \frac{8}{4}$$

$\frac{8}{4}$ equals 2 wholes.

They put aside all the cards they use.

3. Each time a team makes a "whole" set, they put those cards aside in a separate pile. When they can't make any more whole numbers, they return their unused cards to the deck and their turn is over. Each card may be used only ONCE in a turn.

4. When Team One's turn is over, deal Team Two fifteen cards, faceup. Team Two players make all the "whole" sets they can. They keep the cards they use and return the unused cards to the deck.

5. The teams take turns until both have had an equal number of turns and there aren't enough cards left for both teams to have another turn. At the end, the teams count the cards they have kept. The team with the most cards wins the game.

The Make It Equal Game

FOR TWO PLAYERS OR TEAMS

Players make an equation out of their cards.

• •

REMEMBER: An equation is a number sentence in which the amount on one side of the equal sign is EQUAL to the amount on the other side.

How to Play

1. Players decide who goes first. One player shuffles the deck and places ten cards faceup in front of Player One.

2. Player One looks her cards over and arranges them into one

equation. She may add, subtract, or do both. She tries to use as many cards as she can in her equation, since she receives a point for each card she uses.

For example, say her cards are:

She will get 8 points by using the following 8 cards in this equation:

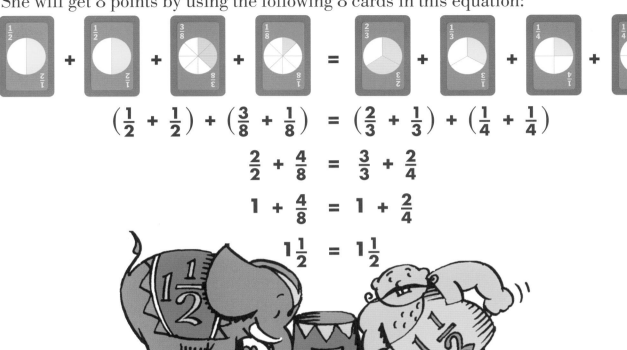

$$\left(\frac{1}{2} + \frac{1}{2}\right) + \left(\frac{3}{8} + \frac{1}{8}\right) = \left(\frac{2}{3} + \frac{1}{3}\right) + \left(\frac{1}{4} + \frac{1}{4}\right)$$

$$\frac{2}{2} + \frac{4}{8} = \frac{3}{3} + \frac{2}{4}$$

$$1 + \frac{4}{8} = 1 + \frac{2}{4}$$

$$1\frac{1}{2} = 1\frac{1}{2}$$

3. Player One keeps the cards she has used and returns the others to the deck. Now Player Two receives ten cards and makes an equation out of his cards. He keeps the cards he uses and returns the others to the deck.

4. In each turn, players make only ONE equation.

5. At the end of the game, players count the cards they kept. The player with the most cards wins the game.

Multiplying Fractions

Multiplying a number by a proper fraction gives a product that's less than the number we started with.

Before we talk about how to multiply fractions, think about this question: What *is* multiplication?

> Doesn't it mean to make MORE groups of a number?

That's what multiplication means *sometimes*. For example, when we multiply 2×6 we make two groups of six each:

$$2 \times 6 = 12$$

Twelve is certainly more than six, so multiplying by 2 does make MORE.

What happens when we multiply a number by 1? Does that also make more?

> I don't think so.

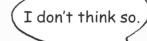

You're right. When we multiply a number by 1, we make only one group of that number.

For example, 1×6 tells us to make one group of six:

$$1 \times 6 = 6$$

Multiplying by 1 doesn't make more. It keeps the amount the same.

We know that multiplying by 2 makes two groups of the number, and that's more than what we started with. And we know that multiplying by 1 makes only one group of the number, which is the same as the amount we started with.

Now, what do you think happens when we multiply by a number that's less than 1?

I don't know.

Well, let's multiply 6 by $\frac{1}{2}$ and see what happens.

To multiply $\frac{1}{2} \times 6$ we make a group that's only one half of 6.

How much would be in that group?

$$6 = $$

$$\frac{1}{2} \text{ of } 6 = $$

$$\frac{1}{2} \times 6 = 3$$

Multiplying by one half ($\frac{1}{2}$) gives us a product that's LESS than what we started with.

"Of" is a key word that means multiply. "What is $\frac{1}{2}$ of 6?" means "Multiply $\frac{1}{2} \times 6$" to find the answer.

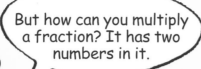

But how can you multiply a fraction? It has two numbers in it.

That's a good question. Actually, it's very simple to multiply fractions.

To begin with, you just have to make sure ALL the numbers you are multiplying are in fraction form.

That means all the numbers have to have a numerator and a denominator.

Fabulous Fraction Fact #10

To multiply fractions, first put all the numbers in fraction form. Then multiply the numerators with each other and multiply the denominators with each other.

Here are the steps to follow:

I don't understand.

Step 1. Make sure all the numbers are in fraction form.

We want to multiply $\frac{1}{2} \times 6$; $\frac{1}{2}$ is already in fraction form, but 6 isn't. To make the whole number 6 into a fraction, we must divide it by 1. $\frac{6}{1}$ is the same amount as 6.

Remember, the bar between the numerator and the denominator of a fraction means "divide." Dividing a number by 1 doesn't change the value of the number.

So ANY number can be written in fraction form by dividing it by 1.

We simply make that number into the numerator and use 1 as the denominator.

Step 2. Multiply the numerators with each other, and put their product as the numerator answer. Then **multiply the denominators** with each other, and put their product as the denominator answer.

$$\frac{1}{2} \times \frac{6}{1} = \frac{1 \times 6}{2 \times 1} = \frac{6}{2}$$

Step 3. Finally, **simplify the product** (the answer) if you can.

$$\frac{6}{2} \div \frac{2}{2} = \frac{6 \div 2}{2 \div 2} = \frac{3}{1}$$

$$\frac{3}{1} = 3$$

Why would I ever want to multiply by fractions?

Multiplying Fractions 1-2-3

1. Multiply all the numerators.
2. Multiply all the denominators.
3. Simplify the answer.

Well, if you happen to be making cotton candy for the concession stand and you want to make only $\frac{3}{4}$ of the recipe because there was too much left over last time, you multiply your ingredients by $\frac{3}{4}$.

Or how about this: your aunt, the famous animal trainer, paid you and your sister $10 for cleaning her tiger's cage. Together you cleaned for 5 hours: you worked 4 hours ($\frac{4}{5}$ of the 5 hours) and your sister worked 1 hour ($\frac{1}{5}$ of the 5 hours). To split the $10 fairly, you should get $\frac{4}{5}$ of the money and she should get $\frac{1}{5}$. Multiply $10 by $\frac{4}{5}$ to see how much you earned.

$$\$10 \times \frac{4}{5} = \frac{10 \times 4}{1 \times 5} = \frac{40}{5} = \$8$$

And your sister gets the rest!

Say you want to build a trapeze for a child, and you want it to be one half the size of the adult trapeze. Multiply the length of the original trapeze bar by $\frac{1}{2}$ to find the length of the new trapeze bar.

Practice Multiplying Fractions

Multiply $\frac{3}{4} \times \frac{1}{2}$

We're going to make a group that is $\frac{3}{4}$ of one half of something. A picture of it might look like this:

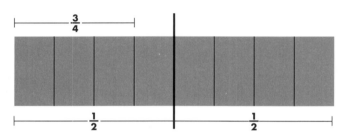

$\frac{3}{4}$ of $\frac{1}{2} = \frac{3}{8}$

Step 1: Multiply the numerators: $(\frac{3}{4} \times \frac{1}{2})$ $3 \times 1 = 3$

Step 2: Multiply the denominators: $(\frac{3}{4} \times \frac{1}{2})$ $4 \times 2 = 8$

$$\frac{3 \times 1}{4 \times 2} = \frac{3}{8}$$

Step 3: Simplify the answer if you can: $\frac{3}{8}$ is already in its simplest form.

To be able to multiply fractions is a very important skill and one you will use a lot. You can start by using it to play the next game.

The Making Less Game

The team with the lower amount wins each turn. At the end, the team with the most cards wins the game.

How to Play

1. Players remove all cards with 12 or 8 in the denominator from the deck.

2. One player shuffles the remaining cards and deals two to each team. Each team multiplies the fractions on their two cards. The team with the lowest amount keeps all four cards.

3. If the teams end up with equal amounts, each team keeps its own two cards.

4. Sometimes teams may have to rename or simplify their answer to find out which is the smaller amount. For example, if one team has $\frac{3}{4} \times \frac{1}{6}$ (which equals $\frac{3}{24}$) and the other team has $\frac{1}{4} \times \frac{1}{2}$ (which equals $\frac{1}{8}$), they both have the same amount because $\frac{3}{24}$ simplifies to $\frac{1}{8}$:

$$\frac{3}{24} \div \frac{3}{3} = \frac{3 \div 3}{24 \div 3} = \frac{1}{8}$$

In that case each team keeps its own two cards.

5. For every turn, each team is dealt two new cards. The teams multiply their fractions. Whichever team has the lower amount wins all four cards.

6. When there are no more cards left in the deck, the teams count the cards they have won. The team with the most cards wins the game.

Challenge: Do not remove the cards with 12 or 8 in the denominator. Use all the cards to play.

Dividing by Fractions

Dividing is the way we find out how many groups of one amount are in another amount.

• •

For example, if we want to know how many groups of 2 are in 6, we divide 6 into groups of 2:

6 ÷ 2 = 🍦🍦🍦🍦
🍦🍦

There are 3 groups of 2 in 6.

6 ÷ 2 = 3

NOTE: Another way to think about it is that 6 ÷ 2 means "Divide 6 into 2 equal groups." How many are in each group? 3.

Since the bar between the numerator and the denominator means "divide," we can also write 6 ÷ 2 this way: $\frac{6}{2} = 3$.

Probably in most of the division problems you've done so far, the answer, called the **quotient** (KWO-shent), has been LESS than the number you started with, called the **dividend** (DIH-vih-dend). 6 ÷ 2 = 3 is like that. The quotient, 3, is less than the dividend, 6.

But when we divide a number by 1, the quotient is the same as the dividend.

For example, to find out how many groups of 1 are in 6, we divide by 1:

6 ÷ 1 =

There are 6 groups of 1 in 6.

6 ÷ 1 = 6

That can also be written this way: $\frac{6}{1} = 6$

When we divide by a number greater than 1, we get a quotient that's *less* than what we started with.

When we divide by 1, we get a quotient that's the *same* as what we started with.

What do you think happens when we divide by a number that's less than 1?

I don't know.

The quotient turns out to be GREATER than the number we started with!

Why?

Let's use the number 12 to show why.

12 ÷ 12 = 1 group of 12

12 ÷ 6 = 2 groups of 6 each

12 ÷ 4 = 3 groups of 4 each

12 ÷ 3 = 4 groups of 3 each

12 ÷ 2 = 6 groups of 2 each

12 ÷ 1 = 12 groups of 1 each

12 ÷ $\frac{1}{2}$ = ?

As the number we divide by, called the divisor (dih-VYE-zer), gets smaller, the quotient gets larger. We can see from the picture that there are 24 groups of $\frac{1}{2}$ in the whole amount 12.

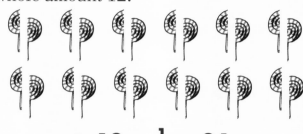

So **12 ÷ $\frac{1}{2}$ = 24**.

Dividing by Fractions

When your divisor is:	Your quotient is:
Greater than 1	Less than the dividend
Equal to 1	Equal to the dividend
Less than 1	Greater than the dividend

Fabulous Fraction Fact #11

If we divide any whole number or fraction by a divisor that's less than 1, our quotient (the answer) will be GREATER than the dividend (the number we started with).

• •

With division we ask how many groups of one amount are in another amount. $12 \div \frac{1}{2}$ asks, "How many groups of $\frac{1}{2}$ are in 12? The answer is 24. There are 24 groups of $\frac{1}{2}$ in 12.

It takes 2 halves to make 1 whole. With 12 wholes, we have 2 halves for every one of those 12 parts—in other words, 12 times two. So $12 \div \frac{1}{2}$ is the same as asking, what number is 12 times two? $12 \times 2 = 24$.

Whenever you're asked to divide by a fraction, you can find the answer by converting it to multiplication.

"**$12 \div \frac{1}{2} = 24$**" is the partner of

"**$12 \times 2 = 24$.**"

Try this one: **$5 \div \frac{1}{4}$.**

How many groups of $\frac{1}{4}$ are in 5?

We know that there are four $\frac{1}{4}$s in every 1 whole. How many $\frac{1}{4}$s are in 5 wholes? 5×4. $5 \div \frac{1}{4}$ is the same as asking, what number is 5 times 4? Here's an example to show how that works.

Say you want to make bags of peanuts to sell. You want $\frac{1}{4}$ pound of peanuts in each bag, and you have a big sack with 5 pounds of peanuts in it. How many bags of peanuts can you make with 5 pounds of peanuts?

To find the answer, you divide 5 by $\frac{1}{4}$. That tells you how many groups of $\frac{1}{4}$ pound are in 5 pounds. Let's do it together:

First we think of 5 pounds as five 1-pound bags. Then we'll divide each of those 1-pound bags into FOURTHS. We end up with 20 fourths, enough to make 20 bags of peanuts.

There's another way to solve $5 \div \frac{1}{4}$. We start by making the whole expression "$5 \div \frac{1}{4}$" into a fraction. Since the bar between the numerator and the denominator means "divide," we can set up $5 \div \frac{1}{4}$ this way:

$$\frac{5}{\frac{1}{4}}$$

Notice that there is a longer line under the 5 than under the 1. That tells us that in this fraction, 5 is the numerator and $\frac{1}{4}$ is the denominator.

$\frac{5}{\frac{1}{4}}$ is a funny-looking fraction, isn't it?

But because we know how to rename fractions, we can rename that funny-looking fraction into one that looks more familiar and is also easier to divide. What's the easiest number to divide by?

One is the easiest number to divide by.

Okay then, let's rename our funny-looking fraction $\frac{5}{\frac{1}{4}}$ into the ONES family.

We'll rename it to a fraction with 1 in the denominator.

But how can we do that?

Look at Fabulous Fraction Fact #3: **When the numerator and the denominator of a fraction are the same number, the fraction equals 1.** So we have to multiply $\frac{1}{4}$ by some number that will change it to $\frac{4}{4}$ because $\frac{4}{4} = 1$.

I know. We can multiply it by 4.

That's it!
First turn 4 into $\frac{4}{1}$, then multiply

$$\frac{1}{4} \times \frac{4}{1} = \frac{1 \times 4}{4 \times 1} = \frac{4}{4}$$

But remember, to rename a fraction, we have to multiply the numerator AND the denominator by the same number. So, if we multiply our denominator by $\frac{4}{1}$, that means we have to multiply our numerator by $\frac{4}{1}$ also.

$$\frac{5 \times \frac{4}{1}}{\frac{1}{4} \times \frac{4}{1}} = \frac{5 \times \frac{4}{1}}{\frac{4}{4}} = \frac{5 \times \frac{4}{1}}{1}$$

Any fraction whose denominator is 1 is equal to the amount in its numerator. So

$$\frac{5 \times \frac{4}{1}}{1} = 5 \times \frac{4}{1} = 5 \times 4 = 20$$

$5 \times \frac{4}{1}$ is the same as 5×4.

And $5 \times 4 = 20$!

The Upside-Down Fraction Division Helper

Now that you know how to divide by fractions the long way, learn how to do it the short way!

Here's a secret: To find the answer to $5 \div \frac{1}{4}$, all we did was multiply $5 \times \frac{4}{1}$! Can you see that $\frac{4}{1}$ is the upside-down version of $\frac{1}{4}$? Upside-down versions of fractions have a special name. They are called reciprocals (ree-SIP-ro-kulz). Reciprocals invert a number's numerator and denominator.

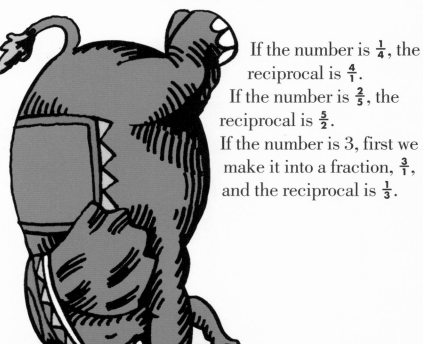

If the number is $\frac{1}{4}$, the reciprocal is $\frac{4}{1}$.
If the number is $\frac{2}{5}$, the reciprocal is $\frac{5}{2}$.
If the number is 3, first we make it into a fraction, $\frac{3}{1}$, and the reciprocal is $\frac{1}{3}$.

The Reciprocal Rule

When you multiply any number by its reciprocal, the product is always 1 whole.

The reciprocal rule is one of the most important rules in math. With help from the reciprocal rule, $5 \div \frac{1}{4}$ becomes $5 \times \frac{4}{1}$, which is the same as 5×4. That's a big shortcut!

The reciprocal rule helps a lot whenever we divide by fractions. Check out Fabulous Fraction Fact #12 to see why.

Fabulous Fraction Fact #12

To divide any number by a fraction, just turn the divisor into its reciprocal and multiply.

• • • • • • • • • • • • • • • • • • • •

Let's test Fabulous Fraction Fact #12 by dividing $\frac{2}{3}$ by $\frac{1}{6}$.

$$\frac{2}{3} \div \frac{1}{6} = ?$$

How many groups of $\frac{1}{6}$ are in $\frac{2}{3}$?

From the illustration, we can see that the answer is 4.

$\frac{1}{6}$	$\frac{1}{6}$	$\frac{1}{6}$	$\frac{1}{6}$	$\frac{1}{6}$	$\frac{1}{6}$
$\frac{1}{3}$		$\frac{1}{3}$		$\frac{1}{3}$	

Now let's work it out with numbers the shortcut way. Since $\frac{1}{6}$ is the divisor, that's the fraction we turn upside down.

$$\frac{2}{3} \div \frac{1}{6} = \frac{2}{3} \times \frac{6}{1}$$

$$\frac{2}{3} \times \frac{6}{1} = \frac{2 \times 6}{3 \times 1} = \frac{12}{3}$$

$$\frac{12}{3} = 4$$

Remember: $\frac{12}{3}$ means "How many groups of 3 are in 12?"

The answer is 4! The shortcut works!

The Great Divide Game

Teams divide their fractions to make whole numbers, then add to see who has the most points.

• •

NOTE: Make sure each team has a pencil and paper to keep score.

REMEMBER: To divide by a fraction, you multiply by its reciprocal.

How to Play

1. One player shuffles the cards and deals ten cards to each team.

2. Teams arrange their cards faceup in front of them. They find pairs of cards to divide that will produce a whole-number answer.

For example:

$$\frac{5}{12} \div \frac{1}{12} =$$

$$\frac{5}{12} \times \frac{12}{1} = \frac{60}{12} = 5$$

or

$$\frac{1}{4} \div \frac{1}{8} =$$

$$\frac{1}{4} \times \frac{8}{1} = \frac{8}{4} = 2$$

3. Players set aside their division pairs and write down their whole-number quotients.

4. After all teams have finished making division pairs and writing down their answers, they add up their quotients to find their scores. The team with the highest score wins that round.

5. Players return their cards to the deck and reshuffle it. Each team receives ten new cards for another round. Teams add up their scores from each round. The first team to get 50 points wins the game.

Congratulations! Now you know how to rename, simplify, add, subtract, multiply, and divide fractions. Let's review.

- **To rename fractions:** Multiply the numerator and the denominator by a ONE fraction (other than $\frac{1}{1}$).

- **To simplify fractions:** Divide the numerator and the denominator by a ONE fraction (other than $\frac{1}{1}$).

- **To add or subtract fractions:** Rename them to a common denominator, then add or subtract the numerators.

- **To multiply fractions:** Follow the three-step rule.

  1. Put all the numbers into fraction form.

  2. Multiply the numerators with each other. That product is the new numerator. Multiply the denominators with each other. That product is the new denominator.

  3. Simplify the answer if it can be simplified.

- **To divide fractions:** Turn the divisor into its reciprocal and multiply using the three-step rule.

You are a full-fledged fraction expert. Have fun with the final game!

The Expert Game

Teams add, subtract, multiply, and divide fractions, then add up their answers to earn points.

• •

NOTE: Addition, subtraction, multiplication, and division are called "operations."

Players need pencil and paper.

How to Play

1. One player removes all cards with 12 or 8 in the denominator, then shuffles the deck and deals each team four cards. Those four cards should each be a different fraction. If a player gets a duplicate card, she trades it for another fraction.

2. In each round, players have four operations to perform. They pick two fractions to add, two fractions to subtract, two fractions to multiply, and two fractions to divide. They write down those four answers. Finally, they add all four answers together to get their score for that round.

3. Of their four cards, players may choose any two for each operation. They may use the same two cards for all or several operations, or they may use a different combination of two cards for each operation.

4. The teams check one another's answers. If a team's answer is correct, that is their score for the first round. If a team has made an error, they correct it and take 2 points from their score for each error made.

5. Deal four new cards to each team for the next round. They add up their answers, check each other's work, and add that total to their first-round score.

6. Teams play three rounds. The team with the highest total score wins the game.

Super expert challenge: Do not remove the cards with 12 or 8 in the denominator, and play this game using ALL the cards.

Fabulous Fraction Facts Review

#1. The bottom number of a fraction is the denominator. It tells how many equal pieces the whole amount has been divided into.

#2. In every fraction, the number above the denominator is the numerator. It tells how many pieces of the whole we are talking about.

#3. When the numerator and the denominator are the same, the fraction equals 1 whole.

#4. To add or subtract fractions, the fractions must all have the same denominator, which means they must all come from the same family.

#5. Two or more fractions can describe the same amount even though their numerators differ and their denominators differ.

#6. Before you can add or subtract fractions with different denominators, you must rename them to a common fraction family to give them a common denominator.

#7. To rename any fraction, we multiply it by a ONE fraction.

#8. A fraction can be simplified if it can be evenly divided by a ONE fraction other than $\frac{1}{1}$.

#9. All whole numbers greater than 1 and all mixed numbers can be written as improper fractions.

#10. To multiply fractions, first put all the numbers in fraction form. Then multiply the numerators with each other and multiply the denominators with each other.

#11. If we divide any whole number or fraction by a divisor that's less than 1, our quotient will be greater than the dividend.

#12. To divide any number by a fraction, just turn the divisor into its reciprocal and multiply.